Got Contentment?
30 Days To A More Contented Life

Joan B. Smith

Acknowledgments

It is virtually impossible to adequately express my thanks to my heart sister and friend, Robin Johnson, for her tireless efforts in helping me put this book together. Without her, it would not have happened. Thank you for your encouragement and hard work!

Many thanks to my husband, Dean, my children, and my parents, who have always been in my corner! Thank you for helping me do what God's called me to do!

Above all, thank you Lord Jesus for all You have given me! I am eternally grateful for Your forgiveness, Your Word, Your presence, and Your strength day to day! You are the Treasure of my life!

Table of Contents

Don't we all want to be satisfied with our lives? Whether we realize it or not, we are all striving for contentment in many different ways. Some of us are working at acquiring **things** for contentment. Others are working hard on careers, trying to achieve a certain level of success for satisfaction. Still others are looking to people and relationships for satisfaction in life. Everyone wants to honestly answer "Yes!" to the question, "Got Contentment?"

It's important to realize that happiness and contentment are **not** the same thing. Happiness is a state of joy that comes from the circumstances of life. Our circumstances can change dramatically from one day to another, significantly altering our level of happiness. On the other hand, contentment is a lasting satisfaction that is not dependent on our circumstances. Even when our circumstances fall into the pits, we can still have an abiding contentment. Jesus said He came to the world to reconnect us to God and make it possible for us to live a contented life, filled with meaning and purpose (John 10:10). So why are so many of us missing out on the life He came to give us? How can we live a more contented life?

First, let's dispel some myths. We are bombarded with empty promises from the media that we will be satisfied with our lives if we will just do some things, usually related to life-changing products and procedures. But these surface changes do not address the deep inner longings within us for meaning and purpose. Having been created in the image of God, we have been created for something far greater than the temporary things of this world. Things can not give us the lasting contentment we are looking for. God is the only true Source of contentment. Everything else is an empty promise and substitute for the real thing. Of course, God wants us to enjoy the blessings he has given us. But are we looking primarily to the blessings, or to the Blessing Giver for contentment?

Jesus mapped out the only way to lasting contentment in Matthew 5. He did not stand up and preach, giving them a "TO DO" list. Instead, He graciously sat down among them and taught them the important truths about the pathway to contentment. Understanding and applying these truths to our lives will naturally lead us to the contentment that God desires for each one of us. Jesus' teaching was then, and is now, revolutionary. The world tells us to work on the outside...to work on whipping ourselves into shape. Jesus dealt with the truth; we must face our need for change on the inside...relying on God and His power to change us.

Having misunderstood Jesus' teaching, known as "The Beatitudes," most of my life, I went on a journey to discover the deeper truths mapped out by Jesus. On that journey, I discovered a hidden treasure of life-changing information that is as relevant today as it was then. It is my prayer that you will examine one nugget of this treasure every day and discover for yourself the only true pathway to contentment!

"Now when he saw the crowds, he went up on a mountainside and sat down. His disciples came to him, and he began to teach them, saying:

'Blessed are the poor in spirit,
for theirs is the kingdom of heaven.
Blessed are those who mourn,
for they will be comforted.
Blessed are the meek,
for they will inherit the earth.
Blessed are those who hunger and thirst for
righteousness,
for they will be filled.
Blessed are the merciful,
for they will be shown mercy.
Blessed are the pure in heart,
for they will see God.
Blessed are the peacemakers,
for they will be called sons of God.
Blessed are those who are persecuted because of
righteousness,
for theirs is the kingdom of heaven.'"

Matthew 5:1-10

"Blessed are the poor in spirit,
for theirs is the kingdom of heaven."

Matthew 5:3

"You're blessed when you're at the end of your rope. With less of
you there is more of God and his rule."

Matthew 5:3 MSG

Day One
Neediness Is A Good Thing

"Apart from me, you can do nothing."
John 15:5

Companion
Reading
John 15:1-11
Deut.
8:17-18

By the age of two, most children have mastered the word "No!" Some stubbornly say, "I can do it myself!" From a young age, our normal tendency is to do everything humanly possible to have things our way. In the world, independence and self-sufficiency are traits to be admired. While we do want to train our children to become independent, they must also understand their dependency on their parents and submit to our authority. In the same way, God tells us that we need to come to the end of ourselves and realize our neediness and utter dependency on Him. He has given us life and everything we need to sustain our lives (Acts 17:24-28). He has created us and knows what is best for us, just as we generally know what is best for our children.

If we were given a choice, few of us would choose to be poor. We generally do not want to be needy. But in Matthew 5:3, Jesus was talking about acknowledging our spiritual neediness. If we submit to God's authority, we will experience His best for our lives. This place of recognized weakness is actually the place of supernatural strength and contentment. Contentment does not come from our trying, but by trusting God.

God is our Source of contentment. We connect with our Source by putting our faith in Christ and trusting His finished work. We can not do anything by self-effort to be at peace with God or to get on the pathway to God's best (Isaiah 64:6). We are poor, needy, and doomed without His grace and mercy.

After connecting our lives with Christ, we then need to stay connected to Him every day, relying on His strength and guidance. Quite often, we realize that we can not save ourselves and be at peace with God, so we do admit our weakness in that area. But then we start trying to live the Christian life in our own strength. It does not take long before we become burned out and frustrated.

Jesus made it crystal clear that if we are disconnected from Him, we can do nothing of lasting value. He wants us to experience complete joy in our journey through life. Without His grace, strength, and guidance we will not experience His best.

What areas of your life are you trying to control yourself without God's help? Have you been trying to be good enough or do enough good for God to be pleased with you? He loves you where you are right now. Will you choose to stop wearing yourself out from **trying** and begin **trusting** Him?

"Blessed is the person who has realized his own utter helpless -ness and has put his whole trust in God."

William Barclay

God, thank You that you want the best for me! Thank you for sending Your Son, Jesus to give me eternal life and to provide a great life for me by showing me how to live day to day. I realize that I am totally dependent on You to guide me on Your pathway to contentment. Help me trust You more every day and rely on Your strength, instead of my own. Amen.

Day Two

Where Is Your Trust?

"Trust in the Lord with all your heart."
Proverbs 3:5

Investment scandals and corporate fraud have frequently made the headlines in recent years. After investing many years on education and careers, people have lost large sums of money in retirement funds due to company mismanagement. While it is important to invest wisely for our future, so many circumstances are beyond our control. With all the uncertainties, what can we invest in with confidence? The Apostle Paul answers this question in Philippians 3.

Paul came from one of the best family trees in Israel. He had a successful career as a Pharisee. He was respected in the community as a moral and extremely religious man. He had invested in all the right things according to the world's standards. Yet, Paul basically said in Philippians 3:7-8 he considered everything he had invested in garbage compared to the time he had invested in his relationship with Christ.

Why was he willing to give up everything and invest primarily in Christ? The reason is that Paul was correctly evaluating his life from an eternal perspective. He knew that his citizenship was ultimately in heaven, and he wanted to invest in things that would last forever, not just for a lifetime. He also knew from experience that God would meet his needs every day and that his future was secure in Christ.

It is easy to get so busy day to day with "making a living" that we loose sight of the importance of "making a life" by investing in our relationship with Christ. It is also easy to get the idea we are the ones in control of

Companion Reading
Philippians 3:4-21
Proverbs 3:1-8
1 Tim. 6:6-10

7

everything. But all it takes is one major "wake up call," like bad news from the doctor or the sudden death of a loved one to show us that we are not in control and we need God's help. If we are already trusting God and acknowledging Him in every area of our lives, we can count on Him to lead us in the right direction to a contented life.

In our fast-paced, materialistic world, we have gotten the wrong impression that packing our life with more will bring contentment. So we pack our lives with fuller schedules, fuller plates, fuller garages, and fuller houses. Trusting in our accomplishments, our money, or our stuff gives us a false sense of security. All it takes is company fraud, divorce, death of a loved one and any number of things that can crumble our security.

When we travel and make hotel reservations, we are given a confirmation number. Having that number guarantees we will have a room when we arrive. When we put our faith in Christ, the Holy Spirit comes into our lives, guaranteeing our reservation in heaven (Ephesians 1:13-14). Our future is secure! So, would it not be wise to invest every day in things that will last forever?

God, I want to trust You with all my heart. I need Your wisdom and direction every day. I recognize that You are in control and I am not. I want to invest in my relationship with You and the things of eternal value. Thank You providing for my needs and my secure future in You! Amen.

"All I have seen teaches me to trust the Creator for all I have not seen."
Ralph Waldo Emerson

Day Three

What's Lacking?

"One thing you lack"
Mark 10:21

Have you ever started making something in the kitchen and realized that you lacked some of the necessary ingredients? For example, it's pretty much impossible to make chocolate chip cookies without chocolate chips. So off to the neighbor's house or to the store we go! When you have your heart set on chocolate, nothing else will satisfy! Obviously, chocolate chips are the most important ingredient. We would not dream of making chocolate chip cookies without the chocolate chips or without a recipe, would we?

But similarly, we live our lives as if we are able to "cook up" a contented life without the key ingredient - God. Contentment is not possible without Him. If we leave Him out, we can have moments of happiness when things are going well, but still lack the missing ingredient to have abiding contentment, regardless of our circumstances.

Companion Reading Mark 10:17-31 Matthew 22:34-40

The rich young ruler in Mark 10 approached Jesus, asking Him for the ingredients to eternal life. He was obviously wealthy and able to have the best of everything that life had to offer. He genuinely wanted to be right with God though and was obviously living a moral life from his responses. The problem was that he wanted a recipe he could follow on his own. He wanted to lead his **own** life, instead of following the Way God mapped out. On the surface, it looked like the rich young ruler had everything. In reality, he had nothing of eternal value, because he was unwilling to submit to the One who created him. Personal wealth and power had first place in his life, not God. Jesus was trying to help the young man see that true wealth is found only in God. Jesus promised that when we surrender everything to God, He gives us more in return than we will ever give up (Mark 10:29-31).

Being right with God is not about following a certain recipe; it's about coming to God on **His** terms…being in a personal relationship with Him. Jesus made it clear that He is the only Way to God (John 14:6). He also made it clear that He is Life…the essential ingredient for eternal life. Thankfully, God wants the best for us and has provided a Way for us to enjoy this life and the one to come in heaven. But we can not get there by stubbornly demanding that God bend to our rules. We have to trust the Way He has mapped out. Jesus is the Way and He lacks nothing!

Are there any serious rivals in your life that God has to contend with? Is there anything you would be unwilling to give up for God?

God, I want You to have first place in my life. With You, I lack nothing that I need for eternal life and contentment day to day. Thank You for guiding my life to bring meaning and purpose. I trust the Way You have mapped out for me. Amen.

"You can aim at heaven and get earth thrown in. Or you can aim at earth and get nothing."

C.S. Lewis

Day Four

Wrong Comparisons

"Let us fix our eyes on Jesus"
Hebrews 12:2

Always looking around, comparing ourselves with others is a dangerous habit. It can also be a trap in which we can get caught. When we compare ourselves with others, it either causes us to be dissatisfied with our lives, or leads to unhealthy pride. We will always be able to find others that appear to be better or worse off than we are, but it is important to remember that we do not know their real circumstances. We can only evaluate based on what we see. And "looks" can be deceiving. Only God can make accurate assessments because He sees the whole picture, including the heart of every person (1 Samuel 16:9).

When we compare ourselves with others, we tend to compare ourselves with those who are morally inferior, instead of with spiritual giants, so we will feel better about ourselves. For example, we might think, "Well, at least I'm not as bad as _____." (You fill in the blank.) This kind of thinking leads to self-righteousness and spiritual pride.

That is the point Jesus made with the comparison of the Pharisee and the tax collector. The Pharisee had become self-righteous, acting as if he had "earned" God's favor and right to heaven. According to Jesus, the tax collector had the more accurate assessment of his spiritual condition. He knew he was in desperate need of God's mercy and forgiveness. We have all sinned and fall short of God's perfect standard of holiness (Romans 3:23). Both the hardened criminal and the most moral person who ever lived are equally in need of God's grace.

Companion Reading Luke 18:9-14 Hebrews 12:1-3

11

We all are! When we "fix our eyes on Jesus," and compare ourselves to His perfection, we should clearly recognize our desperate need for God's help. When we humbly come to God, asking for forgiveness, we can count on His faithfulness to forgive us, and to restore our lives (I John 1:9). On top of that, we have the promise of heaven!

God has created each one of us uniquely different and with a specific purpose. He is not likely to help us be like someone else. He wants us to love and accept ourselves and enjoy the life He has given us. He also wants us to look to Him every day and follow His plan for us. Finding and living in that purpose will bring lasting contentment.

Evaluate your life. Are you constantly comparing yourself with others? Ask God to help you accept your circumstances and be able to celebrate who He's created you to be.

God, I recognize my desperate need for Your mercy and forgiveness. Lord, help me not to compare myself with others. I want to accept and appreciate who You've created me to be. I want You to guide my life every day to lead me in Your will and purpose for my life. Amen.

"Be humble, or you will stumble."

D.L. Moody

"Blessed are those who mourn,
for they will be comforted."

Matthew 5:4

"You're blessed when you feel you've lost what is most
dear to you. Only then can you be embraced by the
One most dear to you."

Matthew 5:4 MSG

Day Five
Sorry Enough to Change

"Live by following the Spirit. Then you will not do what your sinful selves want."

Galatians 5:16 NCV

When my children were younger, and were caught doing something wrong, they would reluctantly say with a whine "Sorry!" But the bad behavior continued. The word "sorry" does not have any value unless the person is genuinely sorry and making an effort to change. Some people say "sorry" because they are actually sorry they got caught. They simply do not want to deal with the guilt or consequences of their sins, and have no intentions of changing.

When we are truly sorry for our sins, we will ask God to forgive us and turn from our sins (II Corinthians 7:10). We have God's promise that He will forgive us of all sin and give us a new start if we truly repent (I John 1:9). Any good counselor will tell you that the first step toward recovery is to admit that you have a problem. Then it is important to take the necessary steps to change.

In Matthew 5:4, Jesus is not saying that we have to stay in a constant state of mourning to be content. He simply wants us to understand the seriousness of sin and to be grieved enough about it to turn away from it. On the surface, sin is appealing, but the result of sin is death (Romans 6:23), robbing us of the best life that God intended for us. Sin leads to brokenness...broken fellowship with God, broken relationships with others, broken emotions, broken dreams, and broken lives. Sin keeps us from God's blessings.

Jesus said He came to the world to give us life... the best possible life (John 10:10). He knew He would have to

Companion Reading
Galatians 5:13-25
Romans 6:1-23

die as a substitute for our sins to provide us with eternal life. The price Jesus paid for our sins was costly, but He joyfully chose death in our place because He knew it would free us from the penalty of sin (Hebrews 12:2).

The world generally minimizes sin and tries to put it in a more positive light. But it is impossible to be cavalier about sin when we realize what it cost Jesus, as well as the devastating effect it has on our lives. If we expect to receive God's best blessings and live a contented life, we must be sorry enough about our sins to change.

Take a brief inventory of your life. Get real with yourself and with God. Ask Him to bring to your mind any sin that you've been unwilling or unable to turn away from. What thoughts did He bring to your mind?

God, I truly am sorry for taking Your grace for granted. Forgive me for getting comfortable with sin. I want to turn from sin every day and walk toward You! Keep me sensitive to Your correction. Amen.

"Sin will take you further than you want to go, and keep you there longer than you want to stay and will cost you more than you want to pay."
Author Unknown

Day Six

Clear Vision

"Woe to me!" I cried. "I am ruined!
For I am a man of unclean lips."
Isaiah 6:5

Companion
Reading
Isaiah 6:1-8
Exodus
3:1-6

I'm OK, You're OK is considered a classic self-help book, selling in excess of ten million copies. It was written in the 1960's by Dr. Thomas Harris. Basically, Harris theorized that everyone has internal voices of the Parent, Adult, and Child (the PAC framework), that play in our heads all the time. He offered a method of reprogramming these voices, to free us up and help us make decisions based on what we really want, not being controlled by outside influences.[1]

According to Harris, then we could live freely as individuals and everyone would be OK. I'd be OK, and you'd be OK. There's one major flaw with this theory. Man has a heart problem, not just a head problem. That heart problem is sin. Until we deal with the sin in our lives, we will not be OK. We all must address the sin in our lives to be OK...with ourselves, with others, but mainly to be OK with God.

Isaiah served as Israel's prophet at a time when most of the nation had turned away from God. Compared to most citizens of Israel, Isaiah stood out as a righteous man. It was Isaiah's job to be God's spokesperson, to confront the people about their sins and warn them about God's impending judgment. Isaiah may have felt fairly good about himself in comparison to everyone else. Even though Isaiah was morally superior to most in Israel, when he saw a clear vision of God, in all His glory, Isaiah was overcome with fear. He realized his utter depravity and sinfulness compared to God's holiness. Isaiah was filled with grief over his own sinfulness and the sinfulness of the people of Israel.

How about you and me? Have we perhaps, like Isaiah, gotten the idea that we are head and shoulders above the crowd when it comes to personal holiness? Or, have we become so desensitized to sin that we have become comfortable with ungodly living? Either way, when we get a clear vision of God's holiness, we will be humbled and grieved over our own sinfulness and the sinfulness of those around us. We will have a more serious attitude toward sin and be less judgmental toward others.

There should be a visible difference between someone living a Christian life and someone who is not. God expects His children to make an effort to live like Him...holy, with godly character (1 Peter 2). He wants us to be radically authentic and different than those who are worldly, not weirdly obnoxious! God wants those who do not know Him to see His love and grace in our lives and as a result to be drawn to Him.

What is different about the way you live your life than someone who does not know God?

Search me, O God, and know my heart; test me and know my anxious thoughts. See if there is any offensive way in me, and lead me in the way everlasting (Psalm 139:23-24). Amen.

"I have hidden your word in my heart that I might not sin against you."

Psalm 119:11

Day Seven

Iffy Thinking

*"Therefore do not worry
about tomorrow."*
Matthew 6:34

Companion
Reading
Matthew
6:24-34
Philippians
4:6-8

Do you have "iffy" thoughts that dominate your life? Thoughts like: "What are we going to do IF that happens? What IF this does not work out? How will I manage IF that happens? IF only I had that! IF only I had not done that!" "What IFS" and "IF onlys" can monopolize out thoughts and paralyze us. Allowing fear and worry to dominate our lives can significantly interfere with our contentment. The presence of continual worry and fear in our lives indicates a lack of trust in God.

Worry and fear can negatively impact our health, our productivity, and our relationships. God expects us to live responsibly and do our best, but He does not want us to be controlled by worry and fear. Genuine concern will move us to act when necessary, but worry and fear immobilize us. We will experience fearful and worrisome thoughts at times, but we do not have to be controlled by them.

The Bible tells us that God did not give us a spirit of fear, but instead power, love, and a sound mind (II Timothy 1:7). Fear and worry are like a broken record, stuck in our heads. As long as we allow the worries to continue playing over and over in our heads, we will remain stuck in the same broken place.

Jesus encourages us to trust instead of fretting about things beyond our control, because He will provide for our needs. The Apostle Paul advised us to replace worry and fear with prayer. Whenever we are worried, the best thing to do is to talk with God.

When we are worried about our children, our finances, our health, or our marriage, the best thing to do is pray. When we talk with God and put our concerns in His hands, He will exchange our worries for His perfect peace. Peace does not require an absence of problems, but rather the presence of God in our lives. God instructs us repeatedly in His Word not to be afraid. In fact, there are at least 365 "fear nots" in the Bible…one for every day of the year!

Transforming our "iffy thinking" into godly thinking happens when we read and meditate on God's Word. It is one of the best prescriptions for decreasing our anxiety level. As we get to know God better and understand His character and faithfulness, we will find it easier to trust Him more and more. God will provide for us and keep us at peace if we keep our minds and thoughts on Him (Isaiah 26:3). He wants us to exchange our "Iffy thoughts" for His perfect peace!

God, forgive me for allowing worry and fear to dominate my thinking. I want to trust You with every detail of my life. I know You are faithful and will provide for all my needs. Help me to remember to pray when I am worried or afraid. Thank You for the peace that You give! Amen.

"A Bible that is falling apart is probably owned by someone who isn't."

E.C. McKenzie

Day Eight

Comfort and Joy

"Praise be to the God and Father of our Lord Jesus Christ, the Father of compassion and the God of all comfort."
II Corinthians 1:3

We were always well stocked with novelty bandaids for boo boos when our children were growing up. Boo boos were a frequent occurrence and a big production. With any injury or fall, my children would come running into the house hunting for me or their daddy to comfort them and help heal their hurts. Covering the boo boo was an absolute necessity, whether the injury was big or small (or even invisible to the naked eye). Our children could not be consoled or comforted until the boo boo was covered. Then, usually, they would joyfully return to their activity... all better.

God announced through the prophet Isaiah hundreds of years before Christ, that His Son, Jesus would eventually come to the world to "preach the good news to the poor...bind up the brokenhearted...proclaim freedom to the captives...release from darkness the prisoners... and comfort all who mourn" (Isaiah 61:1-2). Jesus later identified Himself as that Person that Isaiah described (Matthew 11:4-6; Luke 4:18-19).

God promised that Jesus would comfort ALL who mourn, not just a select few. The Hebrew word for "comfort" used here is also another name for the Holy Spirit. The word "comfort" means to come alongside and walk with through the pain, giving encouragement and hope.

As a parent, we want to comfort our children when they hurt. Our Heavenly Father wants to do the same

Companion Reading
II Cor.
1:3-5
Psalm 32:1-11

21

for all of us. King David described the personal grief and torture he endured when he held onto the unconfessed sin of adultery (Psalm 32:3-4). In contrast, he described the comfort he received from God when he repented (Psalm 32:5-11). God is always ready and willing to forgive our sins and restore our joy, but it is our choice to run to Him and away from our sin.

When we stubbornly hang onto our sins and disobedience, we miss out on God's best, as well as have to suffer the devastating consequences at some point. When we come running to God in mourning and repentance, He will comfort us, and restore our joy (James 4:6-10). Only He can give true comfort and joy!

Who do you run to first for comfort and joy? Is there any sin in your life that you are hanging on to? Will you admit your sin and ask God for His comfort and joy?

"Thy rod and thy staff, they comfort me."
Psalm 23:4

God, forgive me for holding onto sin in my life. Thank You for Your grace and mercy! Help me to understand the seriousness of my sin and always be willing to turn away from it. Thank You for providing me with comfort and joy! Amen.

"Blessed are the meek,
for they will inherit the earth."

Matthew 5:5

"You're blessed when you're content with just who you
are—no more, no less. That's the moment you find
yourselves proud owners of everything that can't be bought."

Matthew 5:5 MSG

Day Nine

Who's The Boss

"We will in all things grow up into Him, who is the Head, Christ."
Ephesians 4:15

Companion
Reading
Ephesians
4:11-16
Matthew
11:28-30

When they were younger, my son and his best friend would occasionally have a disagreement while playing. When things did not go his way, his friend would put his hands on his hips and yell, "You're not the boss of me!" He would grab his toys and head next door to his house.

Jesus said if anyone wanted to be a Christian, they would have to deny themselves and follow Him (Matthew 16:24). The Apostle Paul made it clear Christians need to grow up and follow our Boss, our Head, Christ. We can not just stomp off on our own when things do not go our way if we want to stay on the pathway to contentment. We have to submit to His authority. We can trust Him. He knows what's best and has our best interest at heart.

My best furry friend died a few years ago. He was a Cocker Spaniel named of Cocoa. As a puppy, Cocoa could not have been more undisciplined. He would not listen to a thing. He was off and running after everything that got his attention. But gradually, little by little, he learned to trust and obey me and finally realized the benefits of staying close by my side.

Cocoa and I had a uniquely close relationship. When I said, "Come!" he would jump up and follow me, his master, wherever I went. He always sat at my feet, keeping his eyes glued to me, with an expression that seemed to say, "I adore you! I just love being with you!" I distinctly remember thinking one day, "Lord, I want to adore You the way Cocoa adores me!" Gradually, like Cocoa, over the years of following Christ, I have realized the blessings of companionship with my Master, Jesus.

Jesus said if we would stay connected to Him, and in step with Him, we would learn from Him and live an unburdened, contented life. He is our Master and there are countless treasures to be found when we come to Him, learn from Him, and take His advice and guidance. He promises a life filled with blessings and peace (Matthew 11:28-30). So often, we settle for less than His best by stomping off on our own.

Who is sitting in the driver's seat of your life most of the time? How do you respond when things do not go your way? Will we chose to grow up and let Jesus be the boss of us? If so, we will be well on our way on the pathway to contentment!

God, I know that You have my best interest at heart. Forgive me for blaming You or others when things do not go my way. I want to grow in my relationship with You and trust You every day to guide me in the right direction. Thank You for being so faithful to me! Amen.

"He who does not believe that God is above all is either a fool or has no experience of life."

Statius Caecilius

Day Ten

Weak But Strong

"I will boast all the more gladly about my weaknesses, so that Christ's power may rest on me." II Corinthians 12:9

Companion Reading II Cor. 12:1-10 Isaiah 40:21-31 Phil. 4:12-13

There is a well known deodorant company that boasts about the strength of its product, with the slogan, "Never let them see you sweat!" All of us want to appear confident. Our human tendency is to cover our flaws and weaknesses. That is why Adam and Eve tried to cover their own sinfulness with fig leaves (Genesis 3). They hid from God, the only One with the power and authority to forgive and restore their contentment. At times, we run away from God thinking, "I'm confident I can handle this myself!"

The bookstores are filled with self help books on how to become more confident and successful. Yet, depression is at an all time high. So, what is the problem? Self confidence is based on how we feel about ourselves, as well as on our circumstances. Our feelings and circumstances can fluctuate dramatically from one moment to another, and our confidence goes up and down with it. So how can we overcome feelings of inadequacy and walk every day with confidence?

Jesus said that we need to be meek to have power and provision on earth (Matthew 5:4). Most people think meekness means weakness. Nothing could be further from the truth. Jesus used the word for meek here that pictures a powerful stallion that has been broken and is submitting to the control of its master. Horses do not become less powerful when they are broken. They simply stop using their strength to fight against their master and are able to powerfully move in the right direction.

So meekness implies real strength under control...our abilities under God's control. Meekness does **not** mean submitting to the authority of **everyone**. It does **not** mean being a doormat! It simply means we are submitting to the authority of God.

When we stay focused on the greatness, power, and authority of God, as described by Isaiah, it reminds us of our own helplessness versus the complete capability of God. It gives us confidence to trust in His abilities. Jesus demonstrated perfect meekness when He endured the tortures of the cross. He chose to submit to the authority of God and to die for our sins, which was God's will for His life. Jesus could have called on legions of angels to rescue Him from the cross, but in meekness, he chose to remain where God placed Him for your sake and mine (Matthew 26:52-54). That is perfect strength under God's control! The Apostle Paul testified from personal experience that we **can**, in meekness, trust and follow God confidently because His grace and supply will be more than enough for every circumstance (II Corinthians12:9).

"Depen-dence upon God makes heroes of ordinary people like you and me."

Bruce Wilkinson

God, forgive me for looking to myself and others instead of to You for my confidence. I want to let go of my insecurities and trust You completely. Amen.

Day Eleven

Father Knows Best

*"Does the clay say to the potter,
'What are you making?'"*
Isaiah 45:9

Companion
Reading
Isaiah
45:5-10
Romans
9:19-21

Having a nice hot cup of coffee or tea is one of my favorite things. A pretty mug or tea cup makes the experience even better. Over the years, I've amassed quite a collection of beautiful cups. But, before the cups could fulfill their purpose of making the day better for people like me, it had to go through a complicated process. A tea cup starts out as a big ugly lump of brown or red clay. First, the potter presses and forms the cup into the right shape. After that, he places the cup in a hot oven long enough to keep it from cracking up with use. Then the cup has to sit on the shelf and wait for the next step. After that, the potter adds the finishing touches, glazes it, and returns it to the oven. At that point, the cup looks good and is able to fulfill its purpose.

It's sort of the same for us. God is our Potter and we are the clay. He knew what He was doing when He made us. He also knows exactly what to do to bring out the best in our lives and enable us to fulfill our purpose. The Apostle Paul said that we are God's masterpieces, created to live a life of purpose (Ephesians 2:10).

However, many times, when things heat up and we do not like the circumstances in our lives, we cry out to God to rescue us. Being properly shaped for a purpose is not always a pleasant experience. For some unknown reason, we (clay) get the idea that we know what is best for our lives, more than our Creator (Potter). We tend to take the many blessings He gives us for granted, but blame and question Him when the hard times come into our lives. But our Heavenly Father really does know what is best for our lives. He has promised us that He works out everything for our eternal good (Romans 8:28). Instead of begging to be rescued, a better plan would be to talk with Him regularly and ask for His strength and encouragement to come through stronger. We can also ask Him what He wants us to learn from the experience and thank Him for His presence in difficult circumstances.

When we stop and think about it, we can understand why God compared us to clay. We have been created by the Master Potter. Clay should not have any plans of its own. It is simply pliable and moldable to be shaped however the Master intends. That's what God is looking for…people who are submissive to His will. God can make something beautiful and useful out of clay (people) like that! If we will continually allow God to shape and mold our lives, we will be amazed at what He can do with ordinary clay! His way of shaping our lives has a far superior outcome.

God, forgive me for not trusting You. I want to give You the freedom to mold and shape me according to Your will for my life. Lord, thank You for the promise that You are working everything out in my life for my good. Amen.

Day Twelve

Trust, Don't Take

"Delight yourself in the Lord and He will give you the desires of your heart."
Psalm 37:4

Companion
Reading
Psalm
37:1-40
Genesis
13:1-18

The song, "(You Were) Always On My Mind," was popularized by Elvis Presley and Willie Nelson. If we were to be honest with ourselves, we would have to admit that a better title to that song would be, "I Was Always On My Mind!" The person that is usually on our minds is me, me, me. So much of our time and attention is focused on ourselves. Our human nature plays the questions in our minds, "How does that affect me? What about me?" Our decisions and behavior are driven by "me" thinking.

We come into this world, demanding that others give us what we want and need. All we have to do is watch toddlers playing to realize that we start out with "me/mine" thinking. We seem to have the idea that if we really want something, we need to just grab it. On the surface it appears that it is always someone else who gets all the good stuff, which makes it hard to patiently wait for God to give us what He wants us to have.

But in contrast to our human nature, God has promised us if we will delight in Him, He will give us the desires of our hearts. God's plan for us is always better than ours. When we put God at the center of our lives, trusting Him to provide, He will bless us far more than we can imagine (Ephesians 3:20).

The perfect example of this truth is found in the life of Abraham. Abraham had first choice of the land that God had led him and his family to because he was the eldest in his family. Rather than fight with his family members, Abraham trusted God to provide and humbly let his nephew, Lot, have first choice. Lot was greedy, so he took the land that looked richest on the surface (near Sodom and Gomorrah). We all know how that story turned out! Ultimately it did not pay off for Lot to grab the best for himself without regard for Abraham. As a result, God promised Abraham he would eventually inherit all the land as far out as he could see. He also promised to bless and multiply all of Abraham's descendants. God did eventually fulfill His promise to Abraham in His perfect timing.

God tells us in His Word that when we allow our selfish, sinful nature to dominate our thoughts and actions, we can expect to have a life filled with strife and discontentment. On the other hand, when we allow the Spirit of God to guide our lives, we can experience a life filled with His perfect peace and contentment (Galatians 5:16-23; James 4:1-6). When we allow our sinful nature to compromise our character, God will not bless us. But when we put others first, trust God, and delight in Him, He will bless us and lead us to a life filled with meaning and purpose.

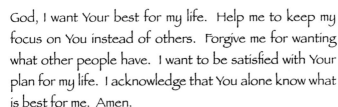

God, I want Your best for my life. Help me to keep my focus on You instead of others. Forgive me for wanting what other people have. I want to be satisfied with Your plan for my life. I acknowledge that You alone know what is best for me. Amen.

"Two natures beat within my breast. One is foul; one is blessed. One I love. One I hate. The one I feed will dominate."

Author Unknown

"Blessed are those who hunger and thirst for righteousness, for they will be filled."

Matthew 5:6

"You're blessed when you've worked up a good appetite for God. He's food and drink in the best meal you'll ever eat."

Matthew 5:6 MSG

Day Thirteen

What Are You Craving?

"My soul thirsts for God, for the living God. When can I go meet with God?"
Psalm 42:2

Companion
Reading
Psalm
42:1-4
1 John
2:15-17

Nothing was very appetizing to me the first two months of my pregnancies. Sometimes just the thought of food, or having to cook certain things would send me over the edge. But after a few months, my appetite returned full force. I was amazed at how good everything tasted and how much food I craved. When we are healthy physically, we should have a healthy appetite. In the same way, when we are healthy spiritually, we should be hungry for spiritual food…time with God, reading the Bible, and prayer.

The psalmist poured out his heart to God when he was depressed, using the analogy of a thirsty deer, in need of water, to express his dire need for God. Blaise Pascal, a 17th century mathematician and theologian, rightly suggested every person is created with a God-shaped vacuum that only He can fill.[2] We were all created with a need for God so we would hunger for a relationship with Him.

What are you hungry for…a bigger house, a nicer car, more money in the bank, a better job, an extreme makeover? What are we spending our time and energy running after? We are being trained to be avid consumers in our world by computers, TVs, and other media resources. They create a hunger and thirst within us to have the newest and best the world has to offer. So, we fill up on the temporary "junk food" from the world that makes us hungry for more. Chasing after worldly things will leave us exhausted and feeling empty in the land of plenty.

John D. Rockefeller was America's first billionaire and

is still considered one of the richest men who ever lived. Someone once asked him how much money it would take for a person to be really satisfied. He responded, "Just a little more."[3]

The Apostle John says clearly that worldly cravings will not give lasting satisfaction. Only God can provide that. Jesus promised if we would put God first in our lives, all the things we need would be provided (Matthew 6:33). Are your cravings leaving you empty or full? What are you chasing after for satisfaction?

God, forgive me for chasing after the things in the world instead of You. I understand that I was created for a relationship with You. I want our relationship the most important priority in my life. Only You can bring complete satisfaction to my life. Amen.

"None of us ever desired anything more ardently than God desires to bring men to a knowledge of himself."

Johannes Tauler

Day Fourteen

Bread That Satisfies

"I am the bread of life. He who comes to me will never go hungry, and he who believes in me will never be thirsty." John 6:35

In my opinion, there is nothing better than the aroma of homemade bread baking in the oven. I can gain five pounds just smelling it! My family always loved getting a fresh loaf of yeast bread from a dear friend of mine in Kentucky. My children acted as if they were receiving the best present ever when I revealed another loaf of "Miss Trish's Bread." It was delicious! But it always left me hungry for more.

In the Beatitudes, Jesus said we would be satisfied if we hungered for righteousness (Matthew 5:6). He later identified Himself as the Bread of Life and Living Water. When we take food and water into our bodies it sustains our lives. When we take Christ into our lives by faith, He sustains our lives for eternity.

Companion
Reading
John
4:7-14
John
6:26-40

Jesus said that we should come to our Heavenly Father every day, asking Him for daily bread - physical and spiritual provisions for the day (Matthew 6:11). Do we hunger and thirst for that daily nourishment from God? He has exactly what we need to meet the demands of every day. He has strength for our struggles, peace for the storms, patience for our trials, and wisdom for the uncertainties in our lives. All of His inexhaustible resources are available to us if we will choose to go to Him every day.

God told Joshua that he would be prosperous and successful if he would meditate on God's Word and put His instructions into practice (Joshua 1:8). The opposite is also true. If we neglect God's Word and fail to put it

37

into practice, we are setting ourselves up for failure and discontentment. The Bible is meant to be our lifetime instruction manual. God can guide us successfully through life with His Word. What or who do we go to for solutions to our problems - self-help books, other people, or God? We live in a demanding world, filled with serious problems. We need God and His Word to help us navigate through the rough waters of life!

It never ceases to amaze me how God tells me exactly what I need to hear, when I need to hear it, through His Word! The Bible is as relevant today as it has been throughout history. It is alive and actively getting right to the heart of every matter in our lives (Hebrews 4:12-13). Do we approach God's Word with a sense of awe and expectancy? Are we hungry and thirsty for God and His righteousness? If so, we will be satisfied!

"Men do not reject the Bible because it contradicts itself, but because it contradicts them."

E.C. McKenzie

God, thank You for giving me Your instruction manual! Your Word is precious to me. Thank You for the promises in Your Word! More than anything else, I hunger for a word from You! Amen.

Day Fifteen
Two-Way Communication

"Call to me and I will answer you and tell you great and unsearchable things you do not know." Jeremiah 33:3

Companion Reading Jeremiah 33:2-3 Psalms 120:1

How fulfilling are relationships in which one person does all the talking? It is probably not very satisfying. Healthy relationships involve mutual give and take. Both people need an opportunity to share thoughts and feelings. Toby Keith had a hit song entitled "I Wanna Talk About Me." His girlfriend obviously talked all the time and never lets him express himself. It is all about her. He's frustrated because he is in a one-sided relationship. Healthy relationships need two-way communication.

Why is it that when we communicate with God, we do all the talking? We have the opportunity to hear from God, our Creator, the One who possesses infinite wisdom, the One who loves us more than we love ourselves, the One who knows the perfect solution to every problem. But instead of listening, most of us tell Him how we want things worked out for us!

I have told one of my sons that if he does not learn to listen, he will never know more than he knows now. Most of us think that we know it all and that nobody knows us better than we know ourselves. Because of that, we think we have the best ideas about how to steer our own lives. But we have very limited knowledge. Only God knows what lies ahead and how to prepare us. The time we spend in two-way communication with God today will help us survive the storms that come tomorrow.

You might say, "How can I listen to Someone when I can not hear Him speak audibly?" I was hoping you would ask that! Most often, God speaks to us through His Word.

The Bible says that the light of God's Word gives insight into our lives and keeps us from stumbling (Psalm 119:105).

Prayer is the other means of listening to God. If we will stop trying to fix things on our own and ask God to speak to us, He will (Psalm 46:10). The Bible tells us to pray continually, not just when we have a major crisis or need. We should stayed tuned in to God throughout the day, and share our concerns with Him (I Thessalonians 5:17). What an amazing thing that we have direct access to God! He is always listening and ready to respond to our needs (Hebrews 4:16). Two-way communication between us and God will deepen our relationship with Him and bring satisfaction to our lives.

⤫⤬⤫

God, forgive me for rushing through our time together, doing all the talking instead of the listening. I desperately want to hear what You want to say to me today and every day. Thank You for providing a way to hear from You! Amen.

"Prayer is a mighty instrument, not for getting man's will done in heaven, but for getting God's will done on earth."

Robert Law

Day Sixteen

Sitting or Serving

*"Mary has chosen what is better,
and it will not be taken away from her."*
Luke 10:42

A father asked his teenaged son to go on an errand for him. The father had car keys in his hand, but had not yet given his son instructions on what to do. Would it be wise to let the son grab the keys and head out on his own, guessing what he should do? Or would it be wiser for him to receive instructions before running the errand? Obviously, the second option is better. This simple illustration reminds us of the importance of listening to God's instructions, before we head out on our own to serve Him.

Companion
Reading
Mark
12:28-34
Luke
10:38-42

The Bible is clear that Christians are called to serve God. Jesus said we could not even be His disciples if we are not willing to deny ourselves and follow Him (Matthew 10:37-38; Mark 8:34). It's clear that Christians are called to obedience and service. It seems odd that Jesus would tell Martha to stop serving and sit down with Him when there was still work to be done. The lesson is: Jesus wanted Martha and us to understand His main priority. It is far more important for us to spend time sitting with Him, before we are prepared for serving Him. We are not told in the Bible to serve the Lord at the expense of knowing Him. Hungering and thirsting for Christ is to be our main priority. When we're growing in our relationship with Christ, we are prepared to follow and serve Him. That leads to great contentment.

When we stop and think about it few, if any, of us decide to have children so we can have more people around the house to help with chores. (If we do, we will be very disappointed.) We have children to add meaning to our lives. We want to love and enjoy our children. God loves us and wants to enjoy a meaningful relationship with each one of us, too. It takes time with our children to teach them and help them grow. We, as parents, do expect our children to be obedient and to contribute to the good of the family when they are able to do so. But it is a parent's desire, more than anything else, to have a close relationship with each one of our children. The same is true for God. He wants us to sit with Him, more than He wants us to serve Him. When we sit with the Lord and learn from Him, we will be prepared to serve Him.

Would Jesus say the same thing to you that He said to Martha? If so, will you make a commitment to Him to sit with Him, before you set out to serve Him?

God, forgive me for neglecting my time sitting with You. I do understand that sitting with You is more important than serving You. Help me to reprioritize my time and to begin putting my relationship with You first. Amen.

"Each of us has a capacity for God and an ability to relate to Him in a personal way. When we do, he brings to us pardon for the past, peace for the present, and a promise for the future."

Ralph S. Bell

"Blessed are the merciful,
for they will be shown mercy."

Matthew 5:7

"You're blessed when you care. At the moment of being
'care-full,' you find yourselves cared for."

Matthew 5:7 MSG

Day Seventeen

Practice Makes Perfect

"Praise the Lord, O my soul, and forget not all his benefits – who forgives all your sins." Psalm 103:2-3

Companion Reading Psalm 103:1-13 Matthew 18:21-35

My daughter Lauren has always had a forgiving heart. Time after time, I have personally seen her extend undeserved forgiveness to someone who has wronged her. As a mother, I have, at times, been indignant about the hurt that others have caused her (the usual stuff that goes on during the teen years) and wanted to get even with the opposition. But usually she wouldn't even say anything negative about the one who wronged her. She does not set herself up as a doormat. She is just a kind and forgiving person. One day I told her I wanted to be just like her when I grew up! God wants **us** to grow up to be like **Him** too...forgiving.

The Jewish rabbis had taught people to forgive those who had wronged them...but only up to three times... no more. So when Peter asked Jesus how many times he should forgive someone, he thought he was being extremely generous to forgive seven times. (It's interesting that Peter asked how many times he should forgive **others**, instead of how many times others should forgive **him**!) Jesus said we should forgive seventy times seven! In other words, we should not even keep a record of offenses. We should be willing to forgive, regardless of how often someone has wronged us.

The parable Jesus used to illustrate forgiveness reminds us that God has forgiven us for an astronomical number of sins, and He wants us to be willing to forgive others too...to reflect His character of mercy and forgiveness. Each one of us has repeatedly sinned against

God. Yet if we truly repent, He will always be faithful to forgive us and wipe the slate clean (1 John 1:9). Realizing how much Christ suffered to provide for our forgiveness should make us more willing to forgive others. When we refuse to forgive, we are preventing God's grace from flowing through our lives out to others.

Jesus included in the Lord's Prayer, "Forgive us our trespasses, as we forgive those who trespass against us" (Matthew 6:12). This does not mean we earn God's forgiveness by forgiving others. Rather, we are told to forgive because God has forgiven us. It doesn't mean we condone wrong behavior. It **does** mean that we give up our rights to hurt others because they have hurt us. God sent His Son to the world to forgive us and make sinful people right with a holy God. Our refusing to forgive interferes with that goal. Forgiveness does not come naturally, especially for those who have been deeply hurt by someone. We usually do not feel like forgiving and we can not do it in our own strength. We must step out in faith and ask God to give us a desire and His power to help us forgive others. As we ask for His help, He will help us practice mercy and forgiveness.

"We are most like beasts when we kill. We are most like man when we judge. We are most like God when we forgive."

E.C. McKenzie

God, thank You for Your grace and mercy! Thank You for forgiving me of all my sins and making me right with You! Your mercy is beyond my comprehension! I want to reflect Your character by forgiving others as You have forgiven me. Amen.

Day Eighteen

Bitter or Better?

"Bear with each other and forgive whatever grievances you may have against one another." Colossians 3:13

Companion
Reading
Genesis
50:15-21
Colossians
3:12-16

All we have to do is pick up a newspaper or turn on the news to get a graphic picture of man's inhumanity to man. We do not often think about it, but there are "walking wounded" all around us...people who have experienced hurt in their lives. Recently I met a middle-aged man from Texas at a conference named Kent, who had experienced the kind of hurt few of us will ever face.

It seems that four years prior, he and his family returned home from dinner and all four of them were shot when they entered their house. His wife and youngest son were killed instantly. He and his oldest son survived. That was bad enough, but nearly two years later, his oldest son was arrested and charged with plotting the murder of his mother, brother and attempted murder of his father — possibly for the family inheritance! His son was found guilty and now sits on death row in Texas.

How can a person ever recover from that kind of extreme hurt? We can't on our own, but God can heal our hurts. The most amazing thing was as Kent told me about his personal tragedy, he said he had forgiven his son and other attackers, but only with God's help. He went on to say he was grateful his son in prison had turned his life over to Christ and was completely changed!

A similar story is told in the Old Testament about the life of Joseph (Genesis 37-50). He was hated by his older brothers because he was his father's favorite. The brothers plotted to kill him, but at the last minute they sold him into slavery. Joseph was taken to Egypt and was eventually placed second in command to Pharoah. Years later, when his brothers came to Egypt to buy food during a famine, they came face to face with their brother, Joseph. Joseph had the power to make them pay for their past injustice. He could have executed every one of them. But instead of being bitter, Joseph had chosen to be better. He forgave his brothers and gave them plenty of food to keep them from starving to death.

Hopefully, most of us will never experience extreme hurt like Kent, or Joseph. But we will all go through some form of hurt and injustice in our lives. Perhaps you have been betrayed by a close friend, endured the unfaithfulness of a spouse, been mistreated by someone you had trusted, lied about by a friend, made fun of... the list goes on. Deep hurts can be crippling. What are you doing with your hurt? Are you holding on to it, or are you giving it to God, asking for His help and healing? God does not want us to become bitter; He wants us to become better. God will make everything right one day. We have His promise that He is working everything, not just some things, out for our eternal good (Romans 8:28).

"Grudges are like hand grenades. It's wise to release them before they destroy you."
Author Unknown

God, You know how deeply _____ has hurt me. I trust You to make things right. Please heal my hurts and give me the desire and the strength to be obedient and forgive, as You have so graciously forgiven me. Amen.

48

Day Nineteen

Are You Forgiven?

"Let us draw near to God with a sincere heart in full assurance of faith, having our hearts sprinkled to cleanse us from a guilty conscience." Hebrews 10:22

Companion Reading
Hebrews 10:19-25
Micah 7:18-19

Imagine if you will a big chalk board covered with a listing of all your past sins. It would take a pretty big blackboard for each one of us for a list like that! The Bible tells us when we put our faith in Christ and repent of our sins, God takes a giant eraser and wipes our slate clean (1 John 1:9). In fact, the Bible says He throws our sins into the deepest part of the ocean and puts up a "No Fishing" sign (Micah 7:19). So, if God no longer holds our sins against us, why do some of us put on scuba gear every day and drag our sins back up, so we can beat ourselves up with them? Wrestling with guilt from the past can be an extremely difficult struggle. Do you find it easier to forgive others, than to forgive yourself? God does not beat us over the head with our past, so why do we?

We accept God's unconditional love and forgiveness when we surrender our lives to Him. After the newness and excitement of this new relationship with Christ wears off and the reality of going through the routines of life sets in, we go back to the same pattern of trying to be "good enough" to earn His favor. We allow our consciences to condemn us and play the tapes over and over in our heads that we are not good enough to deserve God's forgiveness. When we allow guilt from the past to keep us bound up, it prevents us from living in the freedom that Christ came to give us. Our behavior indicates we don't trust Christ's payment for our sins to make us right with God. The writer of Hebrews says this lack of confidence

49

in Christ and His finished work publicly disgraces God's reputation (Hebrews 6:6). It does not give people who do not know Christ the confidence that Christ can help them either if they see us living a defeated life.

The Bible promises us that there is NO condemnation for those who are in relationship with Christ (Romans 8:1). In other words, when we belong to God through faith in Christ, we are free to walk with Him every day without guilt and shame. We aren't free to sin, but free to follow His lead to the best life possible with meaning and purpose. Paul said it was for freedom that Christ set us free. Jesus came to deliver us from real bondage...the slavery of sin (Galatians 5:1). So live free and forgive yourself!

"We often crucify ourselves between two thieves: the guilt of the past and the fear of the future."

Author Unknown

God, thank You for not holding my sins against me! Help me to forgive myself, as You have forgiven me. I want to walk in the freedom Jesus came to give me! Amen.

Day Twenty

Thanksgiving Day

"Give thanks to him and praise his name."
Psalm 100:4

Companion
Reading
Psalm
100:1-5
Luke
17:11-19

When we think of Thanksgiving, many of us reflect on all the delicious food we enjoy that day. Getting together with our families and stuffing ourselves with stuffing is something most of us enjoy. Aside from pigging out, hopefully we reflect on the many blessings God has given us. Instead of having just **one** day a year to focus on everything we have to be thankful for, why not make **every** day thanksgiving day? We are forgiven by faith in Christ and have the promise of heaven, as well as a life of purpose now. We certainly have much to be thankful for! Any blessing He adds beyond that is gravy!

During His early ministry, ten lepers approached Jesus, begging for His mercy and healing. When they trusted Jesus and did what He instructed, they were completely healed! Having leprosy would have been the equivalent of being in the final stages of AIDS today. Lepers merely existed with no hope in the present or for the future.

The unfortunate thing about this miraculous healing is Jesus totally changed their lives, and yet only **one** man out of **ten** came back to thank Him! Before Christ comes into our lives, we are just like that grateful leper… undeserving of God's forgiveness and crippled from the effects of sin. God offers grace and forgiveness, not because we deserve it, but because He loves us. As God's children, we should be even more grateful for God's blessings because we have experienced His grace and mercy.

The Bible tells us Jesus created all things, and His

power continues to hold everything together in our world (Col.1:16-17). Though some refuse to acknowledge God's grace, He continues to show mercy to us all. We who trust Him certainly know Christ keeps our lives from falling apart! Yet, as we go through life, there are so many things we take for granted. It is as if we expect our lives to be filled with blessings only…no difficulties please! Shouldn't we begin every day thanking God for His kindness and end every day praising Him for His faithfulness (Psalm 92:1-2)?

When you think about it, we can never say thank you enough to parents, spouses, friends, and especially to God. There's no way we can repay God for His blessings, but we should thank Him for all He's done. When thankfulness becomes a vital part of our day, our attitude toward life will change. We will gradually become more humble, kind, and loving toward others. God doesn't need our praise, but we need the daily reminder that God is good and His mercy endures forever (1 Chron. 16:34). For that, we should be thankful! Make a list of all the blessings you have experienced in your life, beginning with your relationship with God. Ask God to develop an attitude of gratitude in you.

"It isn't what you have in your pocket that makes you thankful, but what you have in your heart."

E.C. McKenzie

God, forgive me for focusing on what I do **not** have, instead of what I DO have. Thank You for Your grace and mercy! I am forever grateful for Your goodness. Amen.

"Blessed are the pure in heart,
for they will see God."

Matthew 5:8

"You're blessed when you get your inside world—your
mind and heart—put right. Then you can see God
in the outside world."

Matthew 5:8 MSG

Day Twenty-One
Are Your Hands Clean?

"Who may ascend the hill of the Lord? Who may stand in His holy place? He who has clean hands and a pure heart." Psalm 24:3-4

Companion
Reading
Psalm
24:1-10
Proverbs
4:23

Proctor and Gamble introduced Ivory soap in the late 1800's. Ivory soap has always been known for its purity. Before this product was introduced to the public, there were no standards of purity. Soap manufacturers could basically add any ingredient they wanted. Proctor and Gamble starting setting the standards of purity in their industry. They hired an independent lab to analyze Ivory soap, and it was found to be 99.44% pure. Using that information as a marketing tool brought the company huge success. It is interesting to note Mr. Proctor's inspiration for naming the soap, Ivory, came from Psalm 45:8.[+] Psalm 45 is a prophetic passage of Scripture about Christ. Verse 8 describes His robe of righteousness with which He covers His people. Christ gives us clean hands and a pure heart so we may enjoy God's presence and a close relationship with Him.

So how do we clean our hands and purify our hearts? The truth is only God can give us clean hands and a pure heart by faith in Christ. After we are "cleaned up" by Christ, we then follow Him, allowing Him to develop a life of purity in us. There is nothing that we can bring in our hands to the table in this process of purity except trusting and obeying God.

One of the all time classic hymns, entitled "Rock of Ages," was written by Augustus Toplady. The words of this hymn, particularly the first three stanzas, aptly describe our need for Christ in the purity process.

Rock of Ages, cleft for me,
Let me hide myself in Thee.
Let the water and the blood,
From Thy wounded side which flowed,
Be of sin the double cure,
Save from wrath and make me pure.

Nothing in my hand I bring,
Simply to Thy cross I cling;
Naked come to Thee for dress,
Helpless look to Thee for grace;
Foul I to the fountain fly,
Wash me Savior or I die.

Not the labor of my hands,
Can fulfill Thy law's demands;
Could my tears forever flow,
All for sin could not atone;
Thou must save and Thou alone.

"It is a great deal better to live a holy life than it is to talk about it."
D.L. Moody

What are we allowing into our hands and hearts…things that corrupt or things that lead to purity? If we ask Christ to come into our hearts and be in control of our lives, we will be 100% pure because of His presence in us!

God, I realize I can't do anything on my own to have clean hands and a pure heart, except to trust and obey You. Lead me on Your pathway of purity and contentment. Amen.

Day Twenty-Two

Set Apart

"Make them pure and holy through teaching them your words of truth."
John 17:17

Everyone admires people who set themselves apart from mediocrity and devote themselves to excellence. Athletes devote themselves to rigorous training to be a "stand out" in their sport. We love stand out athletes, stand out performers/actors, stand out doctors, stand out inventors/scientists…you get the picture. But we are not quite as thrilled about stand out followers of Christ. Somehow, seeing someone else's complete devotion to Christ may make us feel uncomfortable or inadequate.

God has called His children to be set apart…to be holy because He is holy (1 Peter 1:16). That does **not** mean that He wants us to act "holier than thou" or "fanatically religious." It merely means He wants His children to reflect His character…godly character. We reflect His character when we live a life of love, joy, peace, patience, kindness, goodness, faithfulness, gentleness, and self-control (Galatians 5:22). Our children imitate us and reveal the character we have helped to develop in them. In the same way, we imitate God and His character He has developed in us through our relationship with Him.

Companion Reading John 17:13-19 1 Peter 1:3-25

In His prayer for his followers, Jesus asked His Heavenly Father not to separate us from the world. He wants us to be out in the world (not worldly) to bring His life and light to a dark world (Matthew 5:13-16). What Jesus did request on our behalf was for God to protect us from Satan and to make us more like Himself - sanctified and holy. Jesus asked God to sanctify us through the truth of His Word.

As we meditate on God's Word and put His instructions into practice, God **does** make us more like Christ day by day. It does not happen overnight. It is a life-long process. God leads us to a lifestyle of purity, as we line up everything against the truth of God's Word. Daily application of God's Word has a purifying effect on our hearts and minds. As we read God's Truth, our sin and deception comes to light and it should motivate us to agree with God and turn back in His direction of purity. Living a godly life brings glory to God and should also draw others to Him. Have we been lining our lives up with worldly influences or God's Word? How is our lifestyle different from the world's? Would others be able to identify us as Christians because of the way we live?

God, forgive me for investing too much in worldly things. I realize these things have no eternal value. I want others to see Jesus in me. Create a pure heart in me. Amen.

"Holiness means something more than the sweeping away of the old leaves of sin: it means the life of Jesus developed in us."

I. Lilias Trotter

Day Twenty-Three
Purity Is An Inside Job

"The heart is deceitful above all things."
Jeremiah 17:9

Probably all of us at one time or another have gone to empty the dishwasher and couldn't tell if the dishes were clean or dirty. Then, after putting half the dishes away, we find dirty items that prove the dishwasher had not run yet. The outside of most items **looked** clean, but the dishes were obviously dirty. Because they were dirty, they were not fit for use.

Jesus confronted the religious leaders for trying to appear holy on the **outside**, while being corrupt and dirty on the **inside**. They cared more about **looking** holy than they did about **being** holy. The Pharisees had confronted Jesus in Matthew 15 about His association with sinners. They were more concerned about Jesus getting His hands dirty than they were about helping hurting people.

The Pharisees were very familiar with God's Word, but had refused to be changed by it. Instead, they followed the man-made traditions of religion. It was their responsibility to lead people to God, but they drew attention to themselves instead. They had become a hindrance to people knowing and loving God. Jesus went right to the heart of the matter with His rebuke of the religious leaders. His concern is **not** what we look like on the outside. His concern is for our hearts to be right with Him. Purity is an inside job.

Earlier in His earthly ministry, Jesus taught His disciples the importance of building their lives on their faith in Him…not on the man-made traditions. He gave the chilling prediction of judgment day when the religious person

Companion Reading Matthew 15:1-20 Jeremiah 17:5-10

would come to Him expecting praise and His response will be, "I never knew you. Away from Me, you evildoers." (Matthew 7:21-26).

God is not impressed with our grand gestures of service and sacrifices we make with His name attached to it. What does get God's attention and pleases Him is for our hearts to be right and sensitive to Him...for our motives to be pure (1 Samuel 15:22; Psalm 51:16-17). The true condition of our hearts will be apparent by our behavior, words, and attitudes. If our hearts are pure, we will see and hear from God more clearly. We will see things from His perspective (Matthew 6:22-23).

When our hearts are pure, instead of being critical and judgmental of others, we will be more loving. Instead of being bitter and unforgiving, we will be more understanding and forgiving. When our hearts are right with God, our motivations will be pure. We will be more concerned about being right with God instead of trying to look good for others.

"What's down in the well will come up in the bucket."

Author Unknown

God, change my heart. I want You to develop purity in me. Help me to let go of outward appearances of myself and others. I want more than anything for my heart to be right with You. Amen.

Day Twenty-Four
Living To Please God

"We instructed you how to live in order to please God, as in fact you are living."
I Thessalonians 4:1

Companion Reading
I Thess.
4:1-12
Colossians
3:1-17, 23-24

Are you a "people pleaser"? Do you have trouble saying "no" to others? Do you have trouble saying "no" to yourself? Living to please others, or even to please ourselves is equally exhausting and unfulfilling. God **does** want us to be there for others at His direction, as well as to take care of ourselves. But we were never meant to be totally absorbed with trying to make ourselves or other people happy. That really is an impossible task.

There is a huge difference between doing something for people and doing something for God. Regardless of the situation, God will always have our best interest at heart and will be working everything out for our good (Romans 8:28). He deserves **our** best as well. On the other hand, humans are just that - human. Even when we have the best intentions, people will disappoint us at times, and we will disappoint others too.

We are not perfect; God is. When we come into God's family, He wants us to reflect His character…not perfectly, but with that as our goal. Being in a loving relationship with God motivates us to love others, out of love for Him… living with the goal of pleasing God, not trying to please other people.

As we follow Christ, He will build godly character in our lives as we walk in obedience with Him every day. Over time, He will help us develop an eternal perspective. Instead of looking at the daily demands of life as just a frustration, we will become free to live for Him… our audience of One. As we talk with Him and keep in step with

Him, He will give us rest and peace (Matthew 11:28-30). We tend to complicate our own lives or allow others to push us in a hundred different directions.

Jesus wants us to experience His peace that passes understanding. Think about it. Jesus was on earth for just thirty-three years and in public ministry for only three years. His mission was to change the world, but He was never in a hurry. No one was able to force Him to jump and run at their demands. He lived for an audience of One. He lived to please His Heavenly Father. Who are you living to please? How's that working for you?

God, I want to live to please You. Help me let go of the desire to please others. I want to experience Your peace in my life. Amen.

"We are called to an everlasting preoccupation with God."

A.W. Tozier

"Blessed are the peacemakers,
for they will be called sons of God."

Matthew 5:9

"You're blessed when you can show people how to cooperate
instead of compete or fight. That's when you discover who you
really are, and your place in God's family."

Matthew 5:9 MSG

Day Twenty-Five

Magnetic Personality

"Let the peace of Christ rule in your hearts, since...you were called to peace. And be thankful." Colossians 3:15

There are some metals that can be magnetized by repeatedly coming in contact with a magnet. After the metal is magnetized, it takes on the same properties of the magnet and is able to draw other objects to it as well. The same is true of our relationship with Christ. Maintaining contact with Him will bring His qualities into our lives and others may be drawn to Him through us. One of the main characteristics that we take on when Christ is in our lives is peace. Jesus is The Prince of Peace (Isaiah 9:6-7). He is the only Source of true peace for mankind.

We have peace with God through our relationship with Christ (Romans 5:1-2). Peace with God gives us peace **within**. When we have peace within, we have the Holy Spirit in our lives enabling us to bring peace into our relationships with others. Jesus said we would be content if we were peacemakers and others would recognize us as children of God (Matthew 5:9). He did **not** say that being "peacekeepers" or "peace-lovers" would lead us to contentment. Peace at any cost or keeping our peace when we need to speak up for truth, will not bring true peace. Jesus certainly did not have peaceful relationships with the religious leaders of His day because of His stand for truth. But God **does** want us to bring His peace into our relationships whenever possible.

Before His crucifixion, Jesus instructed His followers not to be troubled or afraid (us included). He promised the Holy Spirit would come after His death to provide guidance and peace ...true peace (John 14:1, 26-27).

Companion Reading Colossians 3:12-17 Philippians 4:4-8

Because of our relationship with Christ, we should always be thankful in all situations...whether difficult or comfortable, because we have everything we need. God wants us to find joy and peace in Him. He promises if we'll trust Him and place our concerns in His hands, He will give us His perfect peace.

Peace **with** God leads to the peace **of** God. Perfect peace in a chaotic, uncertain world is something that others will be drawn to! Are you lacking the peace of God in any situation? Will you choose to place your worries in His hands, so you can receive His peace that passes understanding in return?

Lord Jesus, thank You for the peace You have given me with God! I want to be a peacemaker in my relationships with others. Empower me to bring Your peace to the chaotic world we live in. Amen.

"Peace comes not from the absence of trouble, but from the presence of God."

Alexander Maclaren

Day Twenty-Six

First Steps

"If it is possible, as far as it depends on you, live at peace with everyone."
Romans 12:18

First steps are important to start us moving in the right direction. For example, taking the first steps to get our bodies into shape...taking the first steps to begin a recovery program...and taking the first steps after a divorce or death of a spouse are all big first steps. First steps in **anything** are pretty shaky. We cheered on our children when they took their first steps. It was exciting... but scary. We were afraid they would get hurt. But the more they exercised their legs with walking, the more capable they became.

God wants His children to take the first steps to forgive others and bring reconciliation to their relationships. In fact, Jesus said if there was anyone we were angry with, we should take the first steps to make things right with that person before we worship God (Matthew 5:23-26). Refusing to forgive others obviously interferes with our relationship with God. Jesus further advised if we refused to forgive others, our Heavenly Father would refuse to forgive us (Matthew 6:14-15). That sounds pretty severe, but that is how serious God is about our forgiving others.

Fortunately, while we were still sinners, Christ died for our sins and forgave us (Romans 5:8). He expects us to follow His example and forgive others. We might say, "Let them be the first ones to say they're sorry. It's their fault, not mine!" or "There's no way I can forgive that person for what they did to me! You don't understand how deeply they hurt me!" or "They don't deserve to be forgiven!" All of these may be valid points, but God didn't give us any

Companion Reading Romans 12:9-21 II Cor. 5:11-21

exceptions to this command. He is expecting us to follow in Jesus' footsteps and forgive others as He has forgiven us.

The Apostle Paul did acknowledge that some people are impossible to get along with, no matter how hard we try. God understands that, but He **does** expect us to make the effort to be peacemakers where possible.

Jesus asked God to forgive those who had just nailed Him to a cross. Forgiveness is not a matter of feeling like forgiving. It is a matter of being obedient to God...taking the first steps to be peacemakers. It is humanly impossible to accomplish this on our own. But God can give us the strength to do what He has asked. God will one day make things right. We need to let Him take care of the things that are not fair.

"We are to do acts of kindness to those that least of all deserve it."

William Law

God, what You are asking seems impossible. I know You would not ask me to do anything that was not in my best interest. Give me the strength and the desire to take the first steps to be a peacemaker and forgive others as You have forgiven me. Amen.

Day Twenty-Seven

Divine Unity

"Make every effort to keep the unity of the Spirit through the bond of peace."
Ephesians 4:3

In his last public speech in March of 1799, Patrick Henry said, "Let us trust God, and our better judgment...United we stand, divided we fall. Let us not split into factions..." He died several months following that passionate plea for unity among the states.[5]

The Apostle John recorded Jesus' prayer that He prayed before His arrest and crucifixion. In His prayer, Jesus asked God for several things. But the central request was for God to bring unity to His followers. Jesus was one with His Father, and He prayed for the same oneness among believers. There is supernatural power that comes with unity in the Body of Christ. The enemy is aware of that and has worked continually throughout the history of the Church to disrupt that unity. United we stand, divided we fall.

Unity in the Trinity accomplished redemption for mankind. Unity in the Body of Christ is vital to bring reconciliation between God and those who do not know Him. Christians are to be His peacemakers. If followers of Christ would maintain unity as a main priority, we could have a huge impact on our world for Christ. It is the responsibility of every believer to make every effort to maintain unity and peace in the Church.

How is that going today? Is unity obvious in our churches? Is unity among believers the main priority? Sadly, it does not seem to be the case. Church splits, divisions between pastors and congregations, and inner factions seem to be the rule instead of the exception.

Companion Reading Ephesians 4:1-5 John 17:20-25

The desires of **people** appear to be more important than the desire of **Christ**. Instead of Christians building up other Christians, we seem to be tearing each other down. I know it breaks my heart to see **my** children fighting over insignificant issues. It must grieve our Lord's heart to see the division among His people. All these divisions reflect poorly on God.

Jesus told His followers to love each other as He loved us...unconditionally. His love should be a visible "birth mark" in our lives to show that we belong to Christ (John 13:34-35). If we belong to Christ, we are one with Him and nothing can separate us (Romans 8:35-39). He wants us to be united with other believers to accomplish His purposes. United we stand, divided we fall.

"Lord, make me an instrument of Your peace! Where there is hatred, let me sow love. Where there is injury, pardon. Where there is doubt, faith. Where there is despair, hope. Where there is darkness, light. Where there is sadness, joy. Oh, divine Master, grant that I may not so much seek to be consoled, as to console. To be understood, as to understand. To be loved, as to love. For it is in giving that we receive. It is in pardoning that we are pardoned. It is in dying that we are born to eternal life!"6

"Remember upon the conduct of each depends the fate of all."

Alexander the Great

"Blessed are those who are persecuted because of righteousness, for theirs is the kingdom of heaven."
Matthew 5:10

"You're blessed when your commitment to God provokes persecution. The persecution drives you even deeper into God's kingdom."
Matthew 5:10 MSG

Day Twenty-Eight

Worth Dying For

"For our light and momentary troubles are achieving for us an eternal glory that far outweighs them all." II Corinthians 4:17

Companion
Reading
II Cor.
4:16-18
Hebrews
11:36-38

Church history tells us about a Christian named Polycarp. He committed his life to Christ at a young age and lived a life of total allegiance to Him. Polycarp became a Christian bishop of Smyrna (modern day Izmir, Turkey) in the second century. At the end of his life, he refused to swear total allegiance to Caesar and declare, "Caesar is Lord!" Because of his refusal, Polycarp was stabbed and burned to death for his commitment to Christ. Before his death, Polycarp was quoted as saying, "86 years I served Christ and He has done me no wrong. So, how can I blaspheme my King who saved me?"[7] Polycarp believed that if Christ was worth **living** for, He was certainly worth **dying** for.

Whether we realize it or not, every person who ever lived is living for **something or someone**. Jesus said it like this, "For where your treasure is, there your heart will be also" (Matthew 6:21). In other words, we are investing in whatever means the most to us. Our thoughts, feelings, and will are dedicated to our "first love." So, what in **our** lives is worth living and dying for?

Statistics tell us more Christians have been martyred for their faith in Christ in the last 100 years, than in the first 1900 years since Christ combined! This information does not receive much press. The Body of Christ is dramatically affected by this movement of persecution. As followers of Christ, we need to be alert to such information and give support to those in these difficult, life-threatening situations. The likelihood of persecution of committed

Christians is at an all-time high.

According to "The Christian Post," Islamic Saudi Arabia and communist North Korea are projected as being the world's worst persecutors of Christians in 2008. Both countries forbid the practice of Christianity and impose severe penalties on those who do.[8] In the U.S., we are fairly well protected from this day to day threat, but opposition against us is mounting. Jesus tells us not to be surprised by persecution, but to expect it. He even said persecution leads to contentment (Matthew 5:10). That seems a little odd on the surface, but when we think about it, when we are attacked for our faith, it reminds us that others are reacting negatively to Christ Whom they see in us. His presence in our lives **does** lead to contentment and the promise of heaven! He will be with us and strengthen us to endure any hardship for His sake. Who or what is most important in your life? Is something or Someone worth dying for?

"Those who stand for nothing fall for anything."
Alexander Hamilton

God, I understand when other oppose me because of my faith, it's because of Your presence in my life. Give me the grace and strength to respond in a way that would honor You. Amen.

Day Twenty-Nine

Unusual Celebrations

"The apostles left the Sanhedrin, rejoicing because they had been counted worthy of suffering disgrace for the Name." Acts 5:41

Typically, if we are offered fun...we are in! If we are offered luxury...we are in! If we are offered comfort...we are in! But, if we are offered persecution and suffering, we tend to run in the opposite direction. Our prayers are mostly, "Lord, rescue me! Get me out of this," instead of, "Lord, strengthen me to get me through this!"

Jesus' disciples were arrested, beaten, and threatened because of their stand for Christ. The Jewish Sanhedrin (Supreme Court) instructed them not to make any more public statements about their faith. Yet, the disciples left rejoicing and continuing to testify about the power of Christ. What reason did the disciples have to rejoice? They saw the miracles God performed on their behalf and felt His love and encouragement in the midst of trouble. They had personally experienced the presence of the resurrected Lord, empowering them to endure the toughest circumstances imaginable.

Companion Reading Acts 5:17-42 II Timothy 3:10-17

The same will be true for us! It is never pleasant to be verbally or physically abused for our faith. But we can be encouraged that God will be there with us, encouraging and strengthening us as we endure difficult circumstances. Just as He did for the first disciples, He will work those trials in our lives out for our good.

Jesus never said "if" you are persecuted, but rather, "when" you are persecuted. We shouldn't be surprised when people, who have rejected the authority of Christ, oppose us. We need to remember it is not us others oppose; it is Christ in us (Acts 9:5).

The Apostle Paul, who was once a persecutor of Christians, later reminded his son in the faith, Timothy, all who live a godly life will be persecuted. But, Paul continued to reassure him (and us) Jesus would be there with him in all the tough circumstances. Finally, Paul instructed Timothy to continue growing in the Word so he would be prepared for whatever came his way. We will be prepared if we do the same!

God, I want to trust You with whatever You allow in my life! Lord, guide me as I face opposition so I will always honor You with my response. Amen.

"Jesus has many lovers of His heavenly kingdom, but few bearers of His cross."

Thomas à Kempis

Day Thirty

Heavenly Hope

"But rejoice that you participate in the sufferings of Christ, so that you may be overjoyed when his glory is revealed."
I Peter 4:13

Companion
Reading
I Peter
1:3-9
I Peter
4:1-19

The home is a woman's domain. We go to great lengths and effort to make our homes exactly like we want them. At my house, decorating seems to be a never-ending process. One thing always leads to another! A woman's home should reflect her personal touch.

It is so exciting to think about the lavish décor that Jesus has planned for each one of us in our heavenly mansion! The construction and decorating are in process right now (John 14:1-3). Heaven is being prepared for prepared people!

Jesus promises everyone who puts their faith in Him and pursues righteousness a home in heaven. It will be worth the momentary troubles we might go through on earth to get there. For followers of Christ, we are citizens of heaven (Ephesians 1:13-14). Our life on earth is just a temporary layover before eternity! In the meantime, how we live our lives day to day is important. Following God's purpose for our lives leads to a life of contentment. Scripture tells us to avoid living to fulfill worldly desires. Instead we are to live to accomplish God's will for our lives.

In His final prayer, Jesus said He brought glory to His Heavenly Father by completing the work He was given on earth. One day, each one of us will stand before Christ to give an account for the life **we** have lived (II Corinthians 5:10). What an amazing thing it would be to be able to echo what Christ said, "I have brought you glory on earth by completing the work you gave me to do." If we stay on the Pathway to Contentment, we will be heading in that direction.

Are we pursuing righteousness or worldliness? Are we consumed with fixing up our temporary home on earth, or are we investing in our eternal home in heaven?

God, thank You for preparing my home in heaven! I want to be focused more on my eternal home than my temporary one. Thank You for the heavenly hope You have given through Your Son! Amen.

"Hope can see heaven through the thickest clouds."

Thomas Brooks

Satan's Beatitudes

Blessed are the materialistic and self-sufficient,
   for they are my best representatives!
Blessed are the proud and arrogant,
   for I can convince them never to admit they're wrong.
Blessed are the decadent,
   for I can talk them into anything!
Blessed are the sexually immoral,
   for I can help them snare the innocent.
Blessed are the liars,
   for they do my best work!
Blessed are the pushy and insulting,
   for I can use them!
Blessed are those who gossip and slander,
   for they create division and strife that pleases me!
Blessed are the easily offended, for I can make them bitter!
Blessed are the envious,
   for I can make them dissatisfied with everything.
Blessed are the worriers,
   for I'll convince them not to trust.
Blessed are the fearful and guilt-ridden,
   for I can paralyze them and make them feel unworthy.

The Bible tells us our enemy came to kill, steal, and destroy (John 10:10). He wants to rob us of the contentment Christ came to provide.

Is it really possible to live a contented life in our "pressure cooker" world? Jesus says that it's not only possible, but He mapped out the way to get there in The Beatitudes. Here, Jesus laid out the stepping stones to the treasure of contentment.

First, we humbly come to Christ, recognizing our desperate need for forgiveness.

Then we see the ugliness of our sin more clearly and are sorry enough to turn from it and follow Christ.

After that, we submit to Christ's authority and allow Him to guide our lives every day.

As we learn to trust Christ from our relationship with Him and experience His goodness more completely, we have a greater desire to seek His presence.

We become more like Christ as we grow in our relationship with Him, able to forgive others as He forgave us.

As we follow Christ and His example, our hearts and motives are right with God.

We see things more from Christ's perspective and strive to bring unity and reconciliation to all situations.

We are prepared from our relationship with Christ to face the opposition to our faith with His strength.

Staying on this Pathway to Contentment is possible as we walk closely with Christ!

End Notes

1. Harris, Thomas A. *I'm OK, You're OK*. New York: Harper Collins, 1967.
2. "Quotes by Blaise Pascal." www.thinkexist.com.
3. "Quotes by John D. Rockefeller." www.thinkexist.com.
4. "The History of Ivory Soap." www.essortment.com.
5. "Patrick Henry: Public Speech of March, 1799." www.amnation.com/vfr/archives.
6. "Prayer of St. Francis of Assisi." www.prayerguide.org.uk/stfrancis.htm.
7. "Polycarp." www.wikipedia.org/wiki/Polycarp.
8. Cole, Ethan. "Worst Christian Persecution Expected Saudi Arabia, N. Korea." The Christian Post. January 08, 2008. www.christianpost.com.

About The Author

Joan Smith loves helping others grow in their relationship with God. For 13 years, she served as Teaching Director for Community Bible Study. Joan has also organized and led many conferences, serving as a speaker in small and large group settings. Prior to full-time ministry, she worked in the healthcare industry as a registered nurse and in management. Joan is a Certified Personality Trainer (CPT), and founder of TraitMarks, a business committed to helping people discover their personality traits to improve relationships. She lives in Northwest Atlanta with her husband Dean and has three children.

Joan is honored to hear from her readers. To send comments or questions, or to schedule a speaking event, please contact her directly at: Joan.Smith@TraitMarks.com.

Printed in the United States
202719BV00003B/205-363/P